RED

DOT

PARENTING

HOW TO HELP YOUR KIDS REACH
THEIR SPORTING POTENTIAL

TONY STANGER

POLARIS

PUBLISHING

This edition first published in 2018 by

POLARIS PUBLISHING LTD
c/o Turcan Connell
Princes Exchange
1 Earl Grey Street
Edinburgh
EH3 9EE

in association with

ARENA SPORT
An imprint of Birlinn Limited
West Newington House
10 Newington Road
Edinburgh
EH9 1QS

www.polarispublishing.com
www.arenasportbooks.co.uk

ISBN: 9781909715691

British Library Cataloguing-in-Publication Data
A catalogue record for this book is available on request from the British Library.

Designed and typeset by Polaris Publishing, Edinburgh

Printed in Great Britain by MBM Print SCS Limited, East Kilbride

For my parents, George and Elizabeth.

A tough act to follow.

Our deepest fear is not that we are inadequate.
Our deepest fear is that we are powerful beyond measure . . .

Marianne Williamson

CONTENTS

ABOUT THE AUTHOR

TONY STANGER REPRESENTED Scotland 52 times at rugby union and is currently their joint top try scorer of all time. He scored arguably the most famous try in Scottish rugby history to win the Grand Slam in 1990 and represented the British Lions on their victorious tour to South Africa in 1997. He has a first class honours degree in Applied Sports Science and an Honorary Doctorate from the University of Edinburgh.

After retiring from rugby in 2001, he was a full-time coach for seven years, working at the Leeds Rugby Academy and London Irish. From 2008, he spent seven years as Head of Talent at the Scottish Institute of Sport – a job specialising in understanding the key factors that drive sporting success and how coaches and parents can support young athletes to give them the very best chance of achieving success.

A father of three sporty kids he now runs Stanger Pro, a Talent and Coaching Consultancy working with clients in sport, business and education to help them better understand potential and how to create an everyday approach to development to allow anyone to grow their skills to meet new challenges.

RED DOT PARENTING

IMAGINE THE SCENE. You're driving home from a competition your son or daughter has just competed in. Their training has been going really well and they were buzzing on the way there and looking forward to a successful day. But it was a disaster. Everything that could go wrong, did go wrong. They performed poorly, their coach was fuming and they are now slumped in the back seat of your car looking absolutely gutted.

As a parent who wants to do something to help, what do you say? Do you try to be supportive, *"don't worry, I'm sure it will be better next time"*, or does your own frustration boil over and you find yourself getting stuck in, *"what were you playing at, why did you let them beat you?"*

It can also be just as challenging when things go really well. What do you say then? What sort of impact will a simple *"well done, I thought you were fantastic today"* have on your kids? Is this really the best approach or is there something better?

As a parent of three sporty kids I've faced these challenging situations many times. My kids are my pride and joy and I'm very motivated to do all I can to help them achieve their goals. I call these red dot moments (more on this later) and I know from experience that knowing what to say isn't easy (last weekend my son received a straight red card in a football match for swearing at the referee. As it was an away game, we had a two-hour drive home to talk about it!).

But I also know that I'm in a great position to help my kids because over the last 20 years I've spent a huge amount of time thinking about and studying talent and how to get the best out of sportsmen and women of all ages. The science can be notoriously complex and contradictory and because so much of the crucial information doesn't get to the end user, in our case the parents of young athletes*, I also work with athletes, coaches and parents across a number of sports to understand how to use the science in practice.

In part 1 of this book I will share with you the background evidence you need to know in a very easy to understand way and in part 2 I will show you the simple things you can do when your kids face the ups and downs of sport and you face the, *"what am I going to say now?"* moments.

The focus of the examples in this book will be in sport but you will quickly recognise that this approach will help equip young people to succeed in all areas of their lives.

---

*Throughout this book I will use the word 'athletes' as a generic term to describe people who train and compete in any sport.

THE ROLE OF THE PARENT

BEFORE WE GO any further I want to make one thing clear about the role of parents in supporting sporty kids. You are NOT their coach. Even if you are their coach (which is very possible) you still need to be their parent as well. I want you to understand the role of parents in developing successful athletes is to help support their learning (you also have a crucial role in transportation and funding but that's a challenge for another time!).

And your role is crucial to success ...

> *"Parents are often a better predictor for how their children grow their potential than the children themselves. Behind most top performers you'll find encouraging, stimulating and demanding parents"*

Ankers Rasmusen, *The Gold Mine Effect*

I think we all find it easy to be encouraging but what can parents do to be *stimulating* and *demanding*? Elite sport is very unforgiving and the support athletes receive when they are young has a massive impact on what they achieve in the future.

Why are parents so crucial? Because in sport much of the learning happens BETWEEN competition and training sessions when athletes reflect on what just happened, why it happened and what they could do to make it better next time. I know from experience that kids *sometimes* need a reminder (*stimulating*) to take time to reflect and learn. Parents spend lots of time with their kids and are in a great position to make sure (*demanding*) this process of reflecting and learning becomes a habit the kids drive themselves.

And the good news is you don't have to have all the answers. In fact the less you know about sport the better. You do, however, need to know the questions to ask . . . and when to ask them! To do that successfully there are some things you need to know.

WHAT YOU NEED TO KNOW

"The future depends on what we do in the present"

Mahatma Gandhi

IT REALLY DOES. The habits, skills, techniques and behaviours we develop at key times will have a major impact on what we achieve in the future. And this not only applies to young athletes, but also to coaches and parents. We need to focus our energy on the right things at the right time if we want to be successful in future and in the next few chapters I will share with you the key areas that have been proven to be crucial to long-term success.

But before I do that it's important to understand the things that can happen as your child takes up the challenge of reaching their sporting potential. When kids (or anyone) start something for the very first time there are, in very simple terms, two key challenges parents need to understand.

The first is when the feedback kids receive from doing the activity makes them think they are not good at something. Kids are shocking at comparing themselves to others and, despite what anyone else might say, they use this as their main source of feedback about their ability. So for parents the first challenge you need to help your child avoid is dropping out of sport before they reach a level of competence because they've compared themselves to other kids and convinced themselves, "*I'm no good at this.*"

"*I don't want to go back to gymnastics.*"

"*Why is that, I thought you enjoyed it?*"

"*I do, but everyone is better than me so that means I'm rubbish and I don't want to go back.*"

Sound familiar? Unfortunately this happens all too often and we will discuss in later chapters why this can happen and what you can do about it.

The second challenge you need to think about is when kids get over this level of competence and they get to be quite good at something. This is a dangerous time, particularly if kids compete in a sport where the talent pool, or the number of people competing in their sport or event, might be limited.

When kids start their sporting career they usually compete against other kids of the same age. This does make some sense and is a very traditional approach. But it can limit the quality of the competition they face and there is a danger kids can get away with some weaknesses or bad habits and still be successful, particularly if they are ahead of the game in other areas (like being physically well developed for their age).

Sport is very unforgiving and kids can't afford to have weaknesses in key areas if they want to reach the top.

Making sure young athletes are challenged appropriately (not too much, not too little) is very important in helping to identify the areas where they need to make some changes to avoid the weaknesses and bad habits that might hold them back in the future.

To help you embrace the challenge of avoiding your kids dropping out of sport too early or developing weaknesses in areas crucial to future success, there are six key areas you need to know about:

1. We all develop at different rates

2. ALL skills can be developed

3. It takes time (and motivation!)

4. We need to take responsibility

5. Behaviours are crucial

6. We can't do it on our own

Each area is based on robust science and we will cover them in more detail in the following chapters. In part 2 of the book I will show you how to use this information in practice.

PART ONE

WE ALL DEVELOP AT
DIFFERENT RATES

HERE'S AN IMPORTANT statement I want you to remember. Current performance is **NOT** good at predicting future success. That is, how good we are when you're young is **NOT** a good way of predicting how good we could be when we are an adult.

How do we know? I've looked at the data from a host of different sports and what it tells us is that a huge number of athletes who stood out when they were young don't make the transition from very good junior to very good senior (I'm sure we all know someone from school who was a 'superstar junior' but dropped out of sport soon after).

There are also lots of stories of kids who were OK when they were young, not really standing out, but go on to be amazing athletes.

Ted Ligety was losing races by 7 seconds. And that was just to the other 11-year-olds in his town's ski club. When he tried out for the local developmental racing program they sent him home without a spot. His parents recall that Ted would tell his youth coaches that, one day, he was going to race in the Olympics.

1

They would say, "No, Ted, you have to have a realistic goal". Everyone in the close-knit ski mecca 40 minutes from Salt Lake City knew who the racing prodigies were. Ted Ligety was not among them. High school came and went with many of his friends named to the United States ski team. Ted was not on any coach's list.

'Told to be realistic, Ted Ligety defied his doubters' by Bill Pennington. *The New York Times.* 12/2/14

You may not be too familiar with Ted Ligety but he's a bona fide superstar in downhill skiing. A multiple Olympic and World Champion. One of the best of all time. He didn't really stand out when he was young because **we all develop at different rates** and we see this consistently across sports – six of the US Women's Soccer team who won the World Cup in 2015 were not part of the talent pathway when they were young.

There are also a small number of stories of people who were very good when they were young and still go on to be amazing successful. The golfer Rory McIlroy for example was an Under-10 World Champion. But so were many others over the years who don't play golf anymore!

The other point to make here is that sporting development is a non-linear process. We don't just keep improving at a steady rate. There will be times when kids plateau, times when they improve quickly and other times when they seem to get worse. These stages are all part of the development process every athlete goes through and too often these stages are something that young people are not prepared for.

Why is this important to know? As I mentioned earlier, the trouble is young people (well everyone actually!) are terrible at judging their ability by comparing themselves to others. This is not helpful when we're trying to stop kids dropping out of sport too soon – "*I don't want to go back because they are miles better than me*", or avoiding weakness that will hold them back in future – "*Why should I push myself more at training if I'm beating everyone already?*"

Unfortunately, they are often not helped by the sporting system. As a parent, you will find that many of the sports your kids are involved in still use current performance as the number one selection criteria to 'identify' people with long-term potential. This is not backed up by any evidence. I'm on a quest to change this but in the meantime we do have to accept that it can happen. Rather than throw our arms up in the air we need to do what we can to help our kids see beyond current performance and give them a better picture of what will lead to success in future and encourage them to focus their efforts on that.

As much as we want young people to understand that we all develop at different rates, we also need them to know WHY. There are lots of reasons why this can happen but I've listed below the key things parents need to help their kids to understand:

Maturity

One of the key reasons children develop at different rates is due to physical maturity with those who have grown quicker and are bigger and stronger than others the same age having a significant advantage in many sports. These physical advantages when you're young can be a key factor in competition success and even though some will always be bigger, stronger and faster than others as adults, the impact of these physical advantages are much less at senior level.

In some cases, physical maturity can also be detrimental to performance as kids go through a real growth spurt and struggle to co-ordinate their longer limbs and everything just feels *weird*. They will get used to their *new* body but it can affect their development in the short term.

Emotional maturity may also play a part in how quickly young people develop as they learn to communicate effectively with adults to get important feedback, get the most from training and competition camps when they are away from home and how successfully they balance all the demands in their young lives.

Maturity does even out over time but for young athletes it can vary enormously and has a real impact on their rate of development in sport.

Time on task

If two 14-year-olds have both been in their sport for three years but one has been training once a week and the other has been training five times a week, which one do you think will be better at the moment? Undoubtedly the one who has done more practising.

Does this mean they have better long-term potential? No, it just means they are better at the moment because they have been doing more – what I would call more *time on task*. Kids who do more training tend to develop faster than those who do less.

Working on the things that make the biggest difference

I've seen a lot of people in sport with an outstanding work ethic and capacity to push themselves who are not as successful as they could be because they work hard in areas that don't make a big difference to performance. This is often closely related to the fact that some skills, learning to compete well under pressure for example, are not easy to know how to develop. If you want to be successful, you need to find a way to work on the things that make the biggest difference.

Learning styles

Very closely linked to working on the things that make the biggest difference is the impact of learning styles. Although we all probably have a preference in terms of our learning style …

• some are more solitary and like to work things out on their own while others prefer to work in groups

• some are more visual and like to watch and imitate while others like to physically try the skills to see what they feel like

… it's vital to success that the learning style we use is best suited to the skill we are trying to learn.

Kids need to understand their learning style preference and make sure that how they approach the process of learning important sporting skills is based on **what works rather than what they prefer**. How quickly they find a learning style that works for different skills can vary greatly.

Skills are transferable between sports

Especially physical skills like strength, flexibility or endurance but also other skills like striking a moving object with a racquet or a bat, tactical understanding or being able to perform well under pressure. People who pick things up more quickly than others are usually adapting skills they have learned in other sports, even if they don't recognise it . . .

> *"I've never played badminton before and I did really well."*
> *"Didn't you use to play lots of tennis?"*
> *"Yeah, but I've never played badminton."*

Because skills are transferable it's good to keep playing a number of sports for as long as you can before you decide to focus all your energies on just one. Skills you learn in one sport can transfer easily to a different sport with the added benefit of avoiding kids getting bored or suffering a repetitive-type injury if they specialise in just one sport from a very early age.

Response to training

Without going into the physiological detail, we are all unique and respond differently to different training stimuli. The very best athletes in the same sport don't all train exactly the same way and it can take time to find the training programme that works best for you.

Opportunity

Sometimes we are just in the right place at the right time:

• we get to work with a coach who is expert in developing an area we didn't realise we needed to work on

• we train with a group who are at a level that we find really challenging to live with, but not TOO challenging

• we live near training and get more time to rest and recover

People say you make your own luck and while you can create the opportunities above, it is quite handy if they are there anyway!

Because people develop at different rates and because development is a non-linear process the message for young sportspeople is clear – **DON'T COMPARE YOURSELF TO OTHERS**! Learn from them for sure but don't compare. It won't give you a realistic assessment of what you're capable of.

Any effective development process needs to be **longitudinal** (how can I assess my performance over time?) and **individualised** (what do I need to do to improve?). To do this well we need to understand more about how to develop skills.

ALL SKILLS CAN BE DEVELOPED

THE THING I found most beneficial about working at the Scottish Institute of Sport was the chance to work with real experts in a number of areas, including strength and conditioning, skill acquisition and psychology, to understand the best ways of developing crucial skills.

The good news is that ALL skills can be developed. Advances in coaching and sports science has meant our understanding of how to develop skills has never been better – be that physical skills, technical skills, tactical skills or psychological skills. But even though we know that with hard work we can improve any skill, we also need to understand if there are any 'limits' to how good someone could be.

Here's the one thing I want parents to know about their kids' capacity to develop skills . . .

• Individual characteristics make certain tasks easier or more difficult but **NOT** impossible

We are all different. We are different shapes and sizes, have different muscle fibre types (some help for speed, others for endurance) and have different personalities.

To develop skills effectively, kids need to understand the demands of the task they are trying to get good at and then develop their unique combination of characteristics to give them the best chance of success.

Here's an example. Stefan Holm was an Olympic high jump champion in Athens in 2004 and is a four-times World Indoor Champion. A very successful athlete but would it surprise you to know he is only 5ft 11in tall? This is unusual for the high jump and most of the athletes he competed against were much, much taller. Is being tall an advantage in the high jump? Yes, you are closer to the bar you have to jump over if nothing else!

Does that mean you can't overcome this weakness with strengths in other areas? Apparently not. Stefan Holm believes he probably did twice as many jumps over his career than anyone he competed against and all this training helped him develop very strong and elastic achilles tendons which allowed him to become very 'springy'. As he was smaller than his rivals he was also lighter and focused obsessively on his technique in a sport that he loved. This combination of 'springiness', being technically superb and being lighter than his rivals drove his success.

I'd love to meet Stefan and I'd ask him how often he was told when he was young, "*You're too small to be a high jumper.*" Fortunately, he (and his parents?) clearly understood that being tall wasn't the only factor that was crucial to success in the high jump.

And Stefan Holm's not the only one. Usain Bolt was told (by his coach!) he was too tall to be a 100m sprinter because he would be "*too slow at the start as his long legs would take longer to wind up than the shorter more powerful guys he would be running against*". Turns out this disadvantage could be overcome by his height advantage later in the race when his longer, faster stride became an advantage. As he says in his book, he took 47 strides to cover 100 metres and his opponents took 51. Competitors in the same event with different characteristics. But only one winner!

Now this is not to say everyone can be Usain Bolt or Stefan Holm. If you have weaknesses in too many areas that are crucial to success, then it will be challenging to reach the top in that sport. But if someone loves what they do and wants to continue, should we really be advising them to stop trying?

The other area I want you to help your kids think more about is how to future-proof their skills.

Here's another story to help you understand what this means.

Stephen Curry plays basketball in the NBA in America for the Golden State Warriors. The Warriors won the NBA in 2015 and were beaten finalists in 2016 – driven in large part by the exploits of Stephen Curry.

What was the key to the Golden State Warriors' success? To answer that let's look at how basketball has evolved over the years.

In the 1960s and early 70s the most successful teams had very tall players who could play 'above the rim' and were tall enough to jump above the basket, making it easier to score. So, every team got tall players.

In the 1970s and 80s the 'sky hook shot' brought

success (a side-on, one-handed shot over the top of tall defenders) and the most famous exponent of this was Kareem Abdul-Jabbar. He was soon copied.

In the 1990s and 2000s, Michael Jordan helped bring the 'fade-away jump shot' to prominence – as you shoot you're moving back and away from the defender giving you more 'room' to shoot. It quickly became commonplace.

On a basketball court, there's a three-point line and any shots from outside this line get three points instead of the normal two because, even though players usually get less pressure from a defender, it is a harder shot. In 2016 the 'three-ball' was king and Stephen Curry's success rate from three-pointers (45.6%) was higher than the NBA's average for all shots (41.5%) and was a key factor in the Golden State Warriors' success.

Of course, other teams wanted players who could average 41.5% for three-pointers. Do you think they could find them?

Remember, the future depends on what you do in the present. Stephen Curry recognised that being good at the three-point would give him (and his team) a competitive advantage in the future so he spent countless hours in high school and college practising this shot. It's also interesting to note that at 6ft 3in tall he is small for a basketballer so I'm sure this was partly driven by him looking for ways to use his unique characteristic to best effect in a sport he loved.

Others who hadn't worked as hard on this skill in the past now had to try and catch up and this takes time – especially developing this skill to a level where players can be successful in a match under the greatest pressure.

The message is clear. We need kids to think about the skills they need to future-proof, and make sure they are working on them now.

The role of genetics

I don't want you to get bogged down in the nature vs nurture debate and the role of genetics in sporting performance – I find it fascinating but I know not everyone shares this fascination! However, I have included below a simple summary of the key points about genetics that I feel parents need to know.

The message that young people receive from the media is that ability is 'natural' – you have it or you don't and success is down to having good genes. This isn't accurate but genes do play an important role in what you achieve and I wanted to share with you what scientists currently agree on in terms of the role of genetics in sports performance:

1. Our genes create physical systems which are VERY responsive to different training stimuli – whether that is getting fitter, faster or stronger or developing your reaction time for example.

2. Certain genes do influence the effectiveness of these physical systems but they don't work in isolation and interact with other genes. One gene can't do it all on its own.

3. Genes interact with the environment and can be 'switched' on or off depending on the environment – a field of study called epigenetics.

4. Everyone has a unique combination of genetic strengths and weaknesses in relation to the tasks they are undertaking.

So, we know that no single gene works alone and they create systems that are VERY responsive to training. Even if you do have certain genes that are advantageous in key areas, this advantage can be 'dialled up or down' as the genes interact with the environment – that could be your internal environment and the kind of food you eat or your external environment like whether you live at sea level or at altitude where levels of oxygen in the air are different.

Your combination of genes may give you an initial advantage in a particular area but it is only that, an advantage in one area and not a free pass to a life where everything comes easily.

To be successful athletes need to understand that . . .

• Individual characteristics make certain tasks easier or more difficult but **NOT** impossible

. . . and work with what they have to develop the skills that will bring success in future. They also need to know that 'overnight' success takes time!

IT TAKES TIME
(AND MOTIVATION!)

HAVING SPENT A long time looking, I can't find a story of a successful athlete (or anyone successful for that matter) who has been able to get good really quickly. It takes time and effort and there are no shortcuts.

As you already know, kids don't have to log all these hours in the same sport and there is real merit in not specialising too soon to avoid them getting bored or suffering repetitive-type injuries. Trying a range of different sports is also important to see which one kids enjoy most and I would encourage all parents to let them do this. But be careful. Part of growing up is a process of working out 'who we are' and kids can be tempted to try different sports purely to find the one they are best at compared to others – "*I'm a swimmer and I'm the best in my class.*"

Loving the sport and the type of training, people and competition environment that goes with it is much more important to long-term commitment than early success in a sport you don't really enjoy

There is also real merit in lots of 'unstructured play' with friends and siblings which allows kids to try, learn and improve a range of skills in a fun environment. But however they do it, they do need to put the hours in and be realistic about the amount of time and effort needed to reach the top.

And because it takes time and effort, motivation is crucial.

I've looked in detail at what science tells us about motivation to see if there is one factor that is consistent among successful people. One key thing that gets them up in the morning to do what needs to be done. There isn't. They are all very different.

Some are motivated by proving people wrong. Others are trying to avoid another, less pleasant aspect of their life and time invested in sport helps them 'escape'. Some want fame and fortune. Others become obsessive in their quest to master key skills. Some are inspired by a sporty brother or sister (think the Brownlee brothers in triathlon). Could others just be trying to please their parents?

Although everyone is different, it is important to think about how results influence motivation in young athletes. I don't have actual data on this, but anecdotally from the work I've done with a number of sports, I think around 50% of young athletes (particularly in endurance events like swimming, running, rowing etc.) continue to train and compete when they are young because of early success.

There's no problem with wanting to win and enjoying how it feels when we do, but at some point young athletes will hit a level of competition where they don't always win and improvements in performance are harder to come by. Being motivated to put the hours in because they are winning (something they can't control) rather than because they love it can be very harmful to motivation when this moment comes.

Loving what we do and having a real passion for your sport is crucial in terms of motivation. It's not always clear what drives this passion (there is a world of difference between, "*I love the people in my training squad, we have so much fun*" and "*I like pushing myself until I'm sick!*") but whatever the reason, motivation is crucial as it stimulates people to spend hours and hours engrossed in important practice.

> *"I never looked like being the standout of the family in sport. My brother Bryan was very talented at everything. Rugby, Swimming, Cricket, you name it. He was a proper star from a young age. He was a better cricketer than me coming up through the age groups, but he didn't apply himself as much as I did. He loved life; I just loved cricket."*

> Kevin Pietersen, *KP: The Autobiography*

However, there are two common themes in terms of motivation that are consistent among successful people that are important to understand.

The first is having small improvements along the way to let us know that, irrespective of competition results, the things we are working on will eventually lead to success.

The second is believing we really can be good enough.

Both are crucial to success. Both are not easy to achieve. Both are covered in the following chapters.

WE NEED TO
TAKE RESPONSIBILITY

PROBABLY THE MOST consistent thing I've found in sports men and women who reach the top is they take responsibility for their own development. They don't leave it to someone else.

> *We'll try a drill that she's horrible at – something where she'll start off in the poorer third of the group doing it. Then I'll catch her sneaking practice time to get better at it, so within some period of time, she's one of the best in the group. Some other swimmers, well, they try and they fail at it, and I have to cajole and beg them to try again.*

Bruce Gemmell – Katie Ledecky's coach.

Katie Ledecky is a multiple World and Olympic champion whose success is driven in large part by taking responsibility for her own development, or what scientists call self-regulation.

Research has consistently shown that the difference between experts and non-experts (in a number of areas including sport) is **their ability to self-regulate** by taking responsibility to monitor and control their behaviours to meet their goals.

The research shows there are four key self-regulation skills that make top performers stand out from those who are less successful and I have listed them below:

- Setting specific goals

- Have detailed plans in place

- Continually review and adapt the plan

- Reflection

Athletes will need help and guidance to do this effectively, particularly if they are young. But they do need to develop these skills and from experience, too often young people leave too much of the goal setting, planning and reflection to their coach or parents.

The great news about self-regulation is that these are skills that can be learned and we need to make sure kids keep working on these skills and create habits they can use in all aspects of their life. I'm often asked how soon you should start encouraging kids to take more responsibility and I always say as soon as you can – even if it's just packing their own training snacks or working out what they need to take to a competition (there will be much more on how to do this in the practical section).

But why is taking responsibility for their own development so important? To answer that we need to look again at the four key self-regulation skills.

Set specific goals

When kids are young they might not know what they want to achieve in the future. They might like the idea of being a sporting superstar but aren't sure what this would take or if they would enjoy it.

If kids aren't sure what their long-term goal might be that's OK. What's not OK is not putting in place the short-term goals that keep them focused on the **things you will need to work on now** if you later choose to pursue a career in sport.

These short-term goals act as stepping stones along the way to help kids build the confidence and belief they can be good enough. Being involved in setting short-term goals allows them to take ownership of looking for opportunities to work on key skills and this is particularly relevant in team sports where coaches work with large groups.

When I played rugby, I would listen to the coach as they outlined the session and then identify times in that session that I could focus on the specific things **I needed to work on**. For example, making sure I was up against a smaller, more agile player in defence practice if that was the type of player I would face in the game the following weekend.

I would then have some very specific questions to ask my coach about what I had tried to do, making any feedback very relevant. This approach really accelerates learning but only works if **you know what you need to work on** and consistently look for opportunities to work on these areas in training and competition.

Have detailed plans in place

Once kids have thought about what they want to achieve in both the short and long term, they need a plan that allows them to achieve these goals. As we know this will take time and effort . . .

. . . If things go wrong I need to know why. If we are doing a 200-metre session at this time of year I need to know the reason.

Jessica Ennis, *Unbelievable: From My Childhood Dreams to Winning Olympic Gold*

Why would Jessica Ennis, a world-class athlete who had a team of fantastic coaches around her, need to know why? Could she not just accept that her coaches know what's best? For most people I'm sure a 200-metre running session is probably not the most pleasurable experience you ever go through (particularly in a British winter!) and understanding **why it will help you reach your goals** is crucial in maintaining the motivation you need to get the most out of the session.

Athletes who know **why this is the best plan** for them can more easily push through the tough days and recognise the little successes along the way that build their belief, motivation and confidence (this is another reason why it's important not to purely focus on competition results to assess progress and instead break performance down into its component parts. Your kids won't win every time but there will be lots of little things they do well in defeat that are a sign the plan is working).

Continually review and adapt the plan

I think the biggest challenge your kids will face in developing their skills is deciding when to continue what they are doing because they will get there eventually or when they need to change the plan because it isn't working.

This decision is made more complex because we are all unique and can respond differently to different types of training. A key driver of success is finding a way of training that works best for you and this takes time and accurate feedback.

"How quickly did you recover after that training session?"

"Did you find that approach helped you make more effective decisions in the game?"

"In terms of developing this skill, what has worked well for you in the past?"

The more an athlete takes responsibility for their own learning and is able to **accurately provide feedback on progress**, the more likely they are to help develop a plan that works for them.

Reflection

When I was coaching in rugby it really did used to annoy me when a player would ask, "*What are we working on today coach?*" I might say, "*We're going to build on the work we were doing last time,*" and they would then follow up with, "*What was that again?*"

For some not an ounce of thought had gone into what happened in the last session. They finished, had a shower, did their own thing then turned up again next day waiting to be told what was happening. I must stress this wasn't all players. The ones who were the best learners did think about the previous session and understood **most of the learning happens between sessions** as they thought about what happened and why, what opportunities might be on offer to help them in the next session, what might need more practice and what might need to change.

I'm an introvert and a real reflector and I find it easy to spend time thinking about what just happened and how I can make it better next time. This doesn't mean extroverts can't be good at reflection but they probably won't find it easy and will need to work at it.

I can't stress enough the importance of reflection and the fact that so much learning happens **between** training sessions and competition. No one can do this learning for your kids. They need to take responsibility and get in the habit of doing it themselves.

Hopefully you can see that taking responsibility is crucial to achieving the regular successes kids need to help build motivation and confidence. Believing in themselves is also crucial to long-term success and I will cover this in the next chapter.

BEHAVIOURS ARE CRUCIAL

There's a famous saying which, depending on the search engine you use, goes something like this . . .

If you think you can, or you think you can't. You're probably right

In this chapter, we will look at why your kids might think they can, or think they can't and the crucial role of behaviours in building self-belief. To start, have a look at the diagram below:

Starting at the top, what we believe about our ability will have an impact on our motivation. Our motivation will then have an impact on our behaviours and it's our behaviours which drive the level of performance we achieve. How we performed will then further impact on our belief about how good we can be, which then impacts on our motivation . . . and so on.

So, imagine your son or daughter believes they are not good at something. Their motivation to work on this area can then be limited. You see this lack of motivation in their behaviours as they avoid or show little commitment to the things they need to do to improve, which leads to performance in that area either staying the same or getting worse. If kids try something and performance is poor, *you think you can't* beliefs can be reinforced. (This helps us understand why kids might drop out early from sports they enjoy because of a perceived lack of early success. Or how destructive it can be when someone has early success, believes they are good, and then have this belief challenged when others catch them up.)

What kids believe about how good they can be is crucial to success. Kids can tell you they believe they can do something but you don't know for sure until you see what they do and how much time and effort they commit to doing it (their behaviours).

To help you further understand the impact of beliefs on performance, we need to look at the research of Carol Dweck, an American psychologist from Stanford University, and her work on Fixed and Growth Mindsets. Dweck and her colleagues have been researching this area since the 1970s and it's now being used in practice in education, business and sport. I love her work but it's important to also say there are a number of other psychologists who have found the same effect, they just use different terminology.

Dweck's research centres on whether we believe ability is something about us that is fixed and can't be changed or whether we believe ability is a process of learning and we can get there with effort.

People who believe that talent is predetermined and can't be changed are identified as having a **Fixed Mindset**. They want to show off the things they can do and 'hide' the things they can't. They expect things to come easily and don't work hard on areas they think they are no good at. They can avoid challenges they struggle with and if something does go wrong, they use it as confirmation they are no good – "*I told you I was rubbish at this.*" They ignore feedback that could help them and tend to blame others when things go wrong.

These behaviours impact on performance and decades of evidence from studies by Dweck and others have shown that these behaviours are closely associated with people who underachieve.

People who believe ability is a process of learning and are motivated to learn how to improve are said to have a **Growth Mindset**. They invest effort in areas crucial to success, embrace challenges and understand if they are struggling, they just can't do it **YET**. They see setbacks as part of the learning process and ask for and learn from feedback. They also understand they need to drive their own development (self-regulation) and research has shown that these are the behaviours that are consistent with people who maximise their potential.

Have a think about your kids and the behaviours you

see. Our kids' behaviours, the challenges they embrace and the challenges they might avoid for example, stand out like a sore thumb. But before we discuss this in more detail, I do need to make three crucial points.

Firstly, behaviours are NOT set in stone. The evidence shows us that people can change. This is great news because by focusing on behaviours that can CHANGE, parents can avoid doing the one thing which is arguably the most detrimental in shaping the beliefs of young people – labelling. In society, we love to label people in terms of what they can and can't do. This can be particularly damaging for young people in terms of their beliefs and how committed they are to try and improve.

My wife and I have had to work hard with our kids to make sure they are aware of the labels others might give them – "*people will try and label you but you get to choose if you accept it or not*". I don't promote the use of Dweck's Fixed and Growth terminology because people with a limited understanding of her work can find it too tempting to use it as a label – "*no wonder she can't do it, she's got a fixed mindset*".

Parents need to help kids see their behaviours are a CHOICE and avoid them adopting a label that could hold them back. And be careful you don't become part of the labelling process – "*you're just like me, I was never very good at that at school*". Focus on behaviours that can change – "*do you think you need to work harder on that?*", and avoid labelling at all costs.

Secondly, the behaviours which drive performance are VERY, VERY, VERY task specific. If your kids play tennis, they may really embrace some challenges (keeping focused at training) and not others (playing people who are currently better than them). They may be good at using feedback in some areas (their serve) but not others (their fitness). **Understanding why we might behave in different ways in different situations is the key to changing the behaviours needed to improve performance.**

Thirdly, if beliefs about ability have an impact on the behaviours that drive success, we need to understand where these beliefs come from. The following is not an exhaustive list but from experience these are the key things that shape the beliefs of young athletes:

- The experiences they go through – particularly amazing successes and public failures

- How well they understand their potential and what they need to do to improve

- Other people – particularly coaches, parents and other athletes and how they respond to the ups and downs of the development process

- Society – the message that ability is a natural process is strongly promoted in society

Why parents play such a crucial role in helping kids reach their sporting potential is because they can influence (influence not control) **ALL** these areas. Parents can help kids choose appropriate behaviours as they go through different experiences, they can help them better understand their potential, they can talk through what others have said and how kids use this information and they can even 'promote' stories from the media that are good for kids to hear.

This is all great news. Your kids can change, as parents you can help them by looking for specific areas where a change in behaviour can have the biggest impact on performance and you can influence the key areas where their beliefs come from. There will be much more on how to do this in part 2.

The key message I want you to take from this chapter is that if you can influence the behaviours of your kids, and these behaviours lead to an improvement in performance, this will have a positive impact on their self-belief.

Behaviours are crucial to success and to help you understand what you can do in practice to help your kids, have a look at the table below:

	Behaviours of people **who can underachieve...**	Behaviours of people **who reach their potential....**
Effort	Expect things to come easily	Work hard in areas that make the biggest difference
Challenges	Avoid challenges they struggle with	Embrace challenges – they sometimes can't do it YET
Set backs	Let setbacks confirm they're no good at something	See setbacks are part of the learning process
Feedback	Ignore useful feedback and do what they've always done	Ask questions and use feedback to improve
Ownership	Feel that if things don't work out... it's not their fault!	Understand they need to take responsibility for what happens

YOU ARE HERE

When something happens to your kids, for example they might suffer a bad loss in competition, there are two ways they can go in terms of their behaviours. They could say, *"it wasn't my fault"*, *"I'm not playing them again"* or *"I told you I was rubbish at that"*. Or they could say, *"I need to think a bit more about what I could do better next time"*, *"that was tough, I can't wait to play them again after a bit more training"* or *"that wasn't great but I think I can learn a lot from that"*.

The same experience and two very different responses. I call these red dot moments. Guess which behaviours the research tells us are consistent with the successful people in life when red dot moments come? And who do you think is best placed to help young people through these moments? I'm sure you know the answer to these questions.

Red dot moments are crucial in LEARNING the behaviours that will drive continued success (if kids are not having enough red dot moments, they are not being challenged enough and will miss out on crucial learning opportunities). While it's crucial for young athletes to recognise and drive this process themselves, as we'll see in the next chapter, they do need a helping hand along the way.

WE CAN'T DO IT ON OUR OWN

I WANT TO start this chapter with a cautionary tale.

Unless you're a real hard core golf fan I'm sure you haven't heard of Oscar Sharp. Here he is in his own words taken from an article written about him in the *Golf World* magazine in November 2014.

> *"I'd wake up at 5.30am, and practise my putting. If it was dark, I'd use my phone as a light and work on four-footers. As dawn arrived, I'd work on longer shots. I'd do this for 90 minutes every day before school."*

And this work ethic really drove early success. By age 13 he held a scratch handicap and had become English champion in the Under 14, 15 and 16 age groups in the same year and by age 16 his handicap was plus-three. But this desire to improve provided its own challenges and even though he was working with David Leadbetter, recognised as one of the best golf coaches in the world, he was also talking to another half-dozen coaches, taking bits and pieces from them all and there was a real danger that the advice could be contradictory and confusing and with such a strong focus on practice any technical errors could easily become ingrained.

"But I reasoned that everyone goes through ups and downs, so put my trust in hard work. Surely if I kept working, things would go right eventually."

But results got worse.

"I was confused at this point, as you can imagine. Working hard, not getting the results. It was eating me alive inside. The game was frustrating, but my goals, dreams, drive were intact. I still wanted to become the best and work hard. That never wavered."

Oscar is currently taking a break from the game he loves but he wouldn't want you to feel sorry for him.

"This was self-inflicted. No one forced me or pushed me. It was my hunger to learn, improve, attain those results. It was my dream: I would have done anything to achieve it."

What can we learn from Oscar?

Taking responsibility for your own learning is crucial if you want to get really good. For those who don't play golf, having a plus-three handicap at age 16 means that once you've finished your round you have to **add** three shots to your score.

This story also highlights the need to work hard in the right areas and to do this young athletes need guidance and ongoing support. One of the challenges in golf is that much of the practice is done on your own. Although Oscar was working with some great coaches, there was a danger that when he was left to his own devices there was too much chopping and changing and a lack of clarity about where to focus his efforts (imagine how much more confusing this process could be if parents also add their tuppence worth!). Regular support helps keep young athletes on track.

Coaches, teachers, sports scientists and siblings can all help to provide this guidance and so can parents. But you need to do it in the right way. In the first part of this book I've given you some information which will help you do this. In part 2 I will show you how to use this in practice.

RECAP

BEFORE WE HEAD into the practical section of the book, I wanted to quickly summarise the crucial evidence about ability that parents need to know. I've also provided a summary of the key things you can do to help which I look at in much more detail in part 2.

Evidence	*What parents can do to help their kids*
We all develop at different rates	Don't let your kids *decide* their potential by comparing themselves to others. Instead, help them recognise the small improvements in key areas that help build their confidence
ALL skills can be developed	Help them understand their unique characteristics (height, personality, size etc.) and keep focused on a plan that allows them to develop

the skills they need to be successful in future

It takes time	Think about what motivates your child (why do they love their sport?) and how this could change over time. If your kids are young, encourage them to play with friends and try a range of sports to build their skills without getting bored
We need to take responsibility	Telling kids what to do is not the same as helping them learn. Let them take responsibility and learn for themselves
Behaviours are crucial	*When* the red dot moments happen help your kids to: embrace challenges, overcome setbacks, seek and use feedback to improve and take responsibility for their own development
We can't do it on our own	Help your kids think about and commit time to areas that are crucial to long-term success.

RECOMMENDED READING

IF YOU'RE INTERESTED in learning more about ability and where it comes from there is an absolute mountain of information out there. I've not read it all (but I must be close!) but I did find the following books to be really useful, particularly in terms of my role as a parent, and they are also easy to read. In no particular order:

Mindset: How You Can Fulfil Your Potential by Carol S. Dweck.

Talent is Overrated: What Really Separates World-Class Performers from Everybody Else by Geoff Colvin.

Not in Your Genes: The Real Reasons Children Are Like Their Parents by Oliver James

The Talent Code: Unlocking the Secret of Skill in Sports, Art, Music, Math, and Just About Anything by Daniel Coyle.

The Chimp Paradox: The Acclaimed Mind Management

Programme to Help You Achieve Success, Confidence and Happiness by Steve Peters.

The Gold Mine Effect: Crack the Secrets of High Performance by Rasmus Ankersen.

The Genius in All of Us: Why Everything You've Been Told About Genes, Talent and Intelligence is Wrong by David Shenk.

The Sports Gene: Talent, Practice and the Truth about Success by David Epstein.

The Winner Effect: The Science of Success and How to Use It by Ian Robertson.

Top Dog: The Science of Winning and Losing by Po Bronson and Ashley Merryman.

Bounce: How Champions are Made by Matthew Syed.

Grit: The Power of Passion and Perseverance by Angela Duckworth.

Peak: Secrets from the New Science of Expertise by Anders Ericsson and Robert Pool.

PART TWO

PART TWO

USING WHAT WE KNOW

LET'S START THE practical section of this book with a quick reminder that your role as a parent is to support your child's learning. You are NOT their coach. But you do play a crucial role in helping them learn. Drawing on the information in the previous section, I will show you how to use what we know about ability to help your kids learn and to keep this nice and simple, we will focus on the three areas you can help your kids the most:

1. Help them understand more about ability and WHY they can be successful

2. Help them take responsibility for their own learning

3. Help them recognise and choose the behaviours that lead to success

Having worked with a lot of parents (and using this every day with our kids) the very best way to do this in practice is by asking great questions. Not just asking questions.

Asking GREAT questions. And knowing when to ask them.

Great questions help you understand what your son or daughter is thinking, making it much easier for you to help them. It also encourages them to think about what their options might be, helping them to get into the habit of reflecting and taking more responsibility for their learning.

As you practice and improve you will find great questions become more and more useful. My wife and I have helped our kids get into the habit of looking for opportunities to get more out of their training sessions (they don't always have the undivided attention of their coach) and competitions (when their coach can't make decisions for them) just by using great questions to get them thinking.

So, what does a GREAT question 'look like' and when should you ask them? To understand how to do this there are different types of questions you can use in different situations:

1. General questions – when you're keen to let them choose the direction of the conversation

2. Specific questions – when you want to find out what they're learning in a specific area

3. Guided questions – when you want to talk about their response to a specific situation

4. Follow-up questions – when you want them to

think something through in a bit more detail

5. Call to action questions – when you want to find out what they will do now

I will give you lots of examples of how to use these types of questions in the following chapters and don't worry if you feel you might find this difficult because you know nothing about sport. You won't. In many ways, the less you know the better because you will resist the temptation to 'tell' your son or daughter what to do (from experience, dads are most guilty of this!).

As well as asking great questions, we will also look at how to most effectively praise your kids when they train and compete. How a simple plan can help them (and you!) develop understanding. Some techniques you can use to encourage your kids to reflect more and how you can help them build their self-belief by taking more opportunities to reinforce WHY they can be successful.

Finally, I have included a section on giving feedback. At some point (and quite often if your son or daughter is young) your kids won't be able to think everything through on their own and they will need some ideas about what to do next. This is OK but there are more and less effective ways of doing this and we will cover these in the chapter on how to give feedback.

But first I want to start with how you can help your kids understand more about ability and WHY they can be successful.

HOW TO DEVELOP
UNDERSTANDING

IN THIS CHAPTER I will show you the practical things you can do to help your kids understand WHY they can be successful. Just telling them, *"believe in yourself, you can do it"*, won't work. If you really want them to build self-belief, you need to help them understand WHY they can do it.

"I've been reading an interesting book . . ."

The best place to start is to use the evidence presented in this book and share with your kids what you have learned about ability.

Have a look at the table below. On the left-hand side of the table are the six areas we need them to know about and on the right-hand side are some examples of questions you can use to get them thinking more about ability to develop their understanding. To do this in practice I would start with something like:

"I've been reading a (really interesting!!) book about success in sport and I wanted to talk to you about it."

Then follow this up with ...

> *"One of the key things studies have shown is that people develop at different rates. Have you seen this in your sport?"*

... and let the conversation develop from there and use what you have learned to 'guide' where you need to – *"How do you think maturity impacts of performance when you're young?"*

The evidence tells us . . .   *Ask . . .*

People develop at different rates	*"Have you seen this in your sport?"*
	"Why do you think that is?"
	"Why do you think some people are ahead of you at the moment?"
	"Why do you think you're ahead of some people at the moment?"
ALL skills can be developed	*"What skills will you need to be really good at to be successful in future?"*
	"What is it about you that will

help you develop this skill?"

"What is it about you that you need to work hard on to develop this skill?"

It takes time	*"If it takes a long time to get really good, what will keep you motivated to keep working hard?"*
	"What do you find really helps to keep you motivated?"
	"What other sports or things are you doing that could help you improve?"
Take responsibility	*"Why do you think taking responsibility is so important to success?"*
	"How could you take more responsibility for your own development?"
Behaviours are crucial	*"What behaviours do you think have been shown to be crucial to success?"*
	"What are some of the things

You can't do it on your own   *"If you're not sure what to do, who do you find helps you the most?"*
"What sort of things do people do to help you?"

As you can see there are a mix of general, specific and guided questions in here but I would strongly encourage you to create your own questions. Also, get into the habit of asking these questions regularly to remind them where ability comes from – *"Remember we know that people grow and develop at different rates, have you seen this recently at training?"*

Watch the *Understanding Talent* video

Another way to get you kids thinking about ability is to watch the *Understanding Talent* video we put together when I worked at The Scottish Institute of Sport. It's two minutes long and promotes all the messages you've learned about in this book and is particularly useful for very young athletes. You can find the video by visiting our website – www.stangerpro.com – in our resources section under Parents Top Tips or by typing in 'Understanding Talent video' on YouTube.

Listen to the narrative as the video plays and then

ask your kids questions like the ones below to get them thinking:

- Why do you think people develop at different rates?
- What do you love the most about your sport?
- Do you worry sometimes about how you compare to other athletes?
- Why do you think you are suited to your sport?
- How do you feel if you can't do something?
- Why do you think understanding is so important in being successful?
- Do you think you're good at using feedback to improve?
- What behaviours do you think you need to develop most?

Telling stories

People love stories. Not only do they love them but they remember them (I'm sure if I asked you to think about what you remember from the book so far, real-life stories will be near the top of the list). Share the stories in this book with your kids as it makes the evidence real and much easier to remember.

Also, commit to look for other stories, especially in the sports your kids do, and share them with your kids. It's tempting to think that people who have amazing success have always been successful but this isn't usually the case. Look for stories that illustrate that and share them with your kids and talk about WHY things turned out like they did. Focus on the behaviours that drive success and the importance of how people responded to challenges, setbacks and feedback and their willingness to take ownership. In terms of what to look for, try to find stories of people . . .

- Who didn't stand out when they were young but went on to be very successful
- Who were very successful at a young age but didn't make it
- Who overcame a major setback early on in their career
- Who were successful despite having a weakness in a crucial area – e.g. Swedish high jumper Stefan Holm

Praise

Your kids will want to please you and how you praise them will have a major impact on what they try and do to make you happy. For example, if they feel you are only happy if they win, have a personal best or gain selection for a national programme, then they can feel they've really let you down if that's not what they achieve.

Kids can't control results or selections (as opposed to things they can control like how much effort they put in or their behaviours). If parents focus too hard on outcomes that kids can't control (I've lost count of how many times I've heard a parent offer, "*a fiver a goal*" at football matches!), it can lead to them feeling pressured, unhappy or not equipped to keep learning when the inevitable plateau arrives – all key contributors to early drop-out in sport.

Just to be clear. **I'm not saying good results are a bad thing**. What I'm saying is that parents focusing too hard on results and outcomes is a bad thing. Instead praise them for the effort they have put in and the understanding they are developing on how they could be better in future. Praise from parents is really important and I'm keen you find a way that works for you but I have included some examples below to get you started:

"I know you've been working really hard on this, well done."

"I thought it was awesome you didn't worry about what everyone else was doing and just focused on your own race."

"You've found a way to develop that skill that works for you. Fantastic, that's really good."

"I love the way you took some time to think about what happened last time and tried to make some changes. I'm really proud of that."

"I know you're a bit shy and don't find it easy talking to your coach, but I thought you used the feedback she gave you really well there. That was awesome."

"You were able to put in a great performance under pressure today. Well done, what you have been practising is paying off."

"I know you didn't enjoy losing but I'm really pleased you have taken time to think about what happened and what you can learn from it. Good job."

Remember, your kids want to please you. Use praise to make them see you're happy if they are working hard and learning how to keep improving and you aren't interested in how good or bad they are compared to others at the moment.

A SIMPLE PLAN

IN THIS CHAPTER, I want to show you how to help your kids take more responsibility for their own development – a crucial factor in driving success. If your kids are anything like mine, when you encourage them to take more responsibility, you may very well face, "*why do I need to do this myself, can't you/my coach do it for me?*" So, to help you overcome this challenge I have included below a reminder of why it's important for athletes to take responsibility for their own learning:

1. It allows them to provide accurate feedback to their coaches to create an effective and individualised development plan.

2. They can recognise and take advantage of every learning opportunity in training sessions without having to rely on the direction of coaches.

3. They understand how to make changes in competition when feedback from coaches may be limited.

4. They can work effectively in their own time or with limited supervision.

5. They have given thought to what they want to achieve and know when something is so important to success they can't skip it – especially if it's a tough physical session!

6. They can still be successful if the quality of coaching or parenting is not ideal!

This is not an exhaustive list but I have found that it makes sense to young people in sport and helps keep them motivated to self-regulate consistently.

Now that's out of the way, the focus of this chapter is to share a very simple template you can use to help your kids plan better for success and to give you another opportunity to ask great questions. It's important your kids drive this process themselves but parents also have a key role to play.

Have a look at the planning template on the next page.

What would YOU like to achieve in your sport?			
List ALL the skills you need to be good at to achieve your goal			
List the 3 things YOU need to work on most	The Plan – what will you do to improve in each area?	How will you measure if you're improving?	Reflection – after every session and competition ask ….
			Did I really challenge myself today?
			If something went wrong, how did I try and fix it?
			Did I use the feedback I was given to try and improve?
			Did I take responsibility for making sure I performed well?

Having used this plan many times before I think it's fairly self-explanatory and is designed for kids of any age to work on with the support of their parents to create a plan of the things they need to focus on. They may already have a template they use in their sport which is fine, but if not I use this to great effect in a number of sports.

It's useful because it gets athletes thinking about what they want to achieve, all the things they will need to work on (if they don't enjoy a lot of the training they need to do to improve then maybe being an elite sportsperson is not for them!) and to help identify the things they need to focus on. They may not know their long-term goal and that is fine. But they do need to think about what they would like to achieve in the short term so they can work on and measure something that will give them a lift in confidence and belief that comes with a series of small successes.

I don't want this to be onerous and if your kids don't want to fill in the template that's no problem. I use this approach with my kids but let's just say they're never super keen to write stuff down! This doesn't matter. As long as they know the detail in each area, that's fine. It's also important to note that as things can change quickly, you need to ask them about their plan regularly and I have included below some questions you can use . . .

- *"We spoke a while ago about what you wanted to achieve in your sport; have you had any more thoughts on this?"*

• *"I saw you watching the match on TV yesterday. What sort of skills did you see that you will need to be good at in future?"*

• *"How often do you change the things you are focusing on?"*

• *"What do you find works best for you if you're trying to develop that skill?"*

• *"Who is helping you to measure if that is improving?"*

• *"What are some of the best ways you've found of measuring if you're improving?"*

• *"What opportunities did you have in the session tonight to work on your plan?"*

Reflection

The plan is also a very useful way for you to encourage your kids to get into the habit of reflection after training and competition. I have adapted the reflection questions in the plan so they can be used by parents after every training session or competition:

1. *"What did you find most challenging at training tonight?"*

2. "*What went wrong and how did you try and fix it?*"

3. "*What feedback did you find most useful today?*"

4. "*What more could you do to make the session/ competition better next time?*"

Pen and paper video

In a very similar vein, we put together another video at the Scottish Institute of Sport which helps kids to learn how to plan more effectively. It was designed for athletes to watch with their parents and you can find the video on our website – www.stangerpro.com – in our resources section under Parents Top Tips, or just type in 'how can a pen and paper make you a better athlete' on YouTube.

Training and competition review

One of the trickiest habits to break for parents is to straightaway ask for the score or the outcome after a competition (this is particularly tricky in team sports). As we know, this focuses kids too much on outcomes they can't control (result, Personal Best or scoring a goal etc.) rather than thinking about the signs of individual improvement that help to build belief and motivation.

So what can you do instead? Here's something I have found works really well with our kids. The example below is from football and I start by asking my son what areas of performance (categories) he would like me to ask him about after a game. I have two boys who both play football and although they use different categories (we are all unique!) which change over time, the following have all been consistently on the list:

1. See a pass – did he recognise when a pass was on?

2. Make a pass – was he able to make the pass?

3. Engine – how well did he get up and down the pitch?

4. Hustling – was he strong and persistent in defence?

5. Touch – was he able to get the ball under control on his first touch?

6. Talking – did he communicate with his teammates?

I'm not sure how much you know about football but I asked my boys to watch top level football on TV (they're always happy to do this!) and see if these are the things the very best players are good at. I did this as well because I was keen to learn more but the great thing is these are **their** categories and all my wife and I do is help them to reflect on progress in each area.

The result then matters very little and they can come

away feeling really good even if their team has had a thumping (recognising and making some really good passes can give you a lot of confidence even if your team lost 10-1!).

My youngest is always keen to give himself a score out of 10 in each area which is fine but I do follow up by asking why he gave himself that score (what he did well or could do better). He does ask me for my score and although I do give it, I take the opportunity to ask more questions or give him praise based on effort and understanding:

- *"Just remind me, how much running would a midfielder do to get 10 out of 10?"*

- *"I would give you an 8 for your 'see a pass' because I saw you looking up when the ball was coming to you and I know you've been working hard on that in training."*

- *"I would agree with the 5 you gave yourself for 'engine' because I noticed the time you mentioned where you could have tracked back a bit harder."*

- *"Before I give you a score for communication, how many times can you remember speaking to your teammates?"*

- *"It's tough to give you a score for communication because I was too far away. How much of what you said was technical and how much was trying to encourage others?"*

- *"I agree with your 6 for hustling. How can you work on that at training this week?"*

If you want to be more guided in terms of the categories you use we have also used the following questions to keep our boys thinking:

- *"I was watching a game on TV and there were a lot of one-touch passes – how important do you think what would be to work on in a game?"*

- *"I spoke to your big brother last night and he thinks that communication was really important for him to work on. What do you think about adding that as a category?"*

I'm sure this is clear but I will mention it anyway. You need to **watch** your kids play sport if you want to help them. Not all the time. But regularly. And I mean watch them. You won't find me standing in a queue for a cup of coffee when the game has kicked off or chatting with other parents when my kids are competing because I want to watch what happens so I can ask them great questions afterwards. I'm sure some people think I'm a bit rude but this is important to me.

Motivation

As motivation is so crucial to success, ask your kids what they enjoy most about what they're doing.

"You spend hours at training, what keeps you wanting to go back?"

"Of all the things you need to do to keep improving, is there anything you don't really enjoy?"

It may sound strange to say people need to take responsibility for their own motivation but it's important to ask kids to keep reflecting on why they love their sport (as we said earlier, there is a world of difference between, "I love the people in my training squad, we have so much fun" and "I like pushing myself until I'm sick!") and to help them look for signs when their motivation may be low or when the things they used to love about their sport change. For example:

• They've always been motivated by winning and are now going through a spell where they lose regularly.

• They love the people they train with but now need to work with another group they don't know who will challenge them more.

If kids know what motivates them and how this can change as they experience the ups and downs life throws at them then you're in a good place to do something about it. When kids are young there are lots of factors that affect motivation (puberty, results, deselection, peer pressure etc.). Having parents on hand to help them navigate the motivation minefield is important.

An easy one to finish

Be honest. How many of you pack your son or daughter's training bag? Or chase them to make sure they're ready to leave on time? Or ask their coach a question they could have asked themselves?

No matter how old they are, it's important kids start the process of taking responsibility as soon as possible. One of the best ways parents can help is to make sure kids learn what they need to do to prepare for training and competition by packing what they will need themselves.

And no matter how shy they are it's important to start to learn the communication skills they need to get accurate feedback and talking to their coach is a great way to start.

In our house we tell our kids what time we need to leave and expect them to have everything ready. They know this is their responsibility and is part of performing well and although they have all forgotten something fairly significant in the past (my daughter once went to an all-day swimming gala with nothing to drink) they haven't done it again!

You might think you're helping by doing things for them (I find from experience that mums are most guilty of doing too much for young athletes!) but they learn much less about what they need to do to prepare to train and compete at their best so **avoid the temptation**.

RED DOT MOMENTS

WE KNOW BEHAVIOURS are crucial to success. We also know that behaviours are very specific to the task you are undertaking and are not set in stone – people can change. The longer you have been behaving in a certain way the harder it is to change. But you can change.

Before we look at how parents can help their kids to choose the behaviours most likely to lead to success, let's look again at the red dot table below and the behaviours you might see.

	Behaviours of people **who can underachieve...** ⬇	Behaviours of people **who reach their potential....** ⬇
Effort	Expect things to come easily	Work hard in areas that make the biggest difference
Challenges	Avoid challenges they struggle with	Embrace challenges – they sometimes can't do it YET
Set backs	Let setbacks confirm they're no good at something	See setbacks are part of the learning process
Feedback	Ignore useful feedback and do what they've always done	Ask questions and use feedback to improve
Ownership	Feel that if things don't work out... it's not their fault!	Understand they need to take responsibility for what happens

(YOU ARE HERE marker overlaid between the Set backs rows)

Red dot moments will happen to your kids. How much they learn from them will depend on how they respond. As a parent, it's important to have an idea of the kind of red dot moments your kids may face and to help you I have included some examples of the type of things that can happen as they engage in sport:

• not being as good or being much better than others they train with

• picking up a skill more quickly or more slowly than others

• facing a period of very tough, physically demanding training

• training – finding a session difficult that others seemed to find easy

• results – better than expected or a lot worse than expected

• being selected or deselected

• now competing in an event or category with much older and better athletes

• results – beating people who used to beat you

• results – getting beaten by people you used to beat

- feedback – *"you're the best 14-year-old I've ever seen"*

- feedback – *"sorry, you're not going to make it"*

- plateaus – working hard but not improving

- rapid improvement or unexpected drops in performance

- being asked to do additional work in your own time

- performing well or poorly under pressure at a big competition

- the feedback they receive is minimal and poor quality

- being well prepared or ill prepared for competition

There are lots of other examples of what can happen which are relevant in different sports but hopefully this is useful as a start point. And remember, red dot moments are not just when things go wrong. Your behaviours when things are going really well are just as important to long-term success – *"my coach has asked me to work on my technique but I'm not going to because I'm winning easily already"* is less likely to lead to success than, *"that was a great result but I'm going to think about what I can do now to keep myself ahead of the competition"*.

What now?

Now we know the behaviours to look for and the kinds of situations that can happen in sport, here's the process I want you to use to help your kids when red dot moments happen:

1. What happened?

2. How do they feel about what happened?

3. Do they understand why it has happened?

4. What are they going to do now?

5. Praise

6. Follow-up

What happened?

They may tell you what happened, or you may witness it first-hand, but don't leave it to chance to find out – ask.

How do you feel about what has happened?

By finding out how they feel about what happened (their emotional response) you can learn a lot about how you can help. For example:

• They feel frustrated – are they being realistic about how long it will take to improve?

• They feel embarrassed – are they worried what others think and may start to avoid the things they can't do?

• They feel angry – are they angry at themselves or are they looking to blame others for what has happened?

• They are even more determined – have they seen this as a bit of a wake-up call?

There are lots more options but hopefully this gives you an idea of why this question is so important.

Do you understand why it has happened?

Once you're clear on what has happened and how your kids feel about it, follow up by asking your kids, "*Why do you think that happened?*" This really is important as it's where you will start to understand more about the behaviours they choose:

• Was it because of something they did or didn't do or are they blaming others?

• Do they see this as part of the learning process and a challenge to be embraced of something they will try and avoid in future?

• Is it a setback which they see as part of the learning process or has it reaffirmed something they feel they have never been very good at?

• Have they tried to use the feedback to find ways to improve (even if the feedback is delivered in a bit of a rant) or have they already convinced themselves to keep doing what they've always done?

They may not always know why some things happen but either way it's important to get them thinking about it. Use guided questions if they are struggling but don't worry too much if they don't know. The most important thing is what they are going to do now.

What are they going to do now?

This is where you can use 'guided' questions to positively influence the behaviours of your kids. It does take a bit of time and effort to do this well but it's well worth it in the end. A simple, "*what will you do now?*", can work really well but often a more 'guided' approach is needed to get the most from the situation:

• "*I know you found this really challenging. What are some of the ways you can keep challenging yourself in this area so you have a better chance of being successful next time?*"

- *"Remember we talked about how important setbacks are in terms of your learning. What do you think you will do differently in future?"*

- *"I wouldn't like hearing that either but let's take a minute to talk this through. I do think they are only trying to help so tell me one thing they said that you feel you should think about a bit more?"*

- *"I agree it would be good if you could improve a bit faster. What could you do in your own time that will help you do this?"*

With practice you will find 'guided' questions that work well for you but as rule of thumb it's always useful to use them to reinforce the behaviours that have been shown to drive success.

Praise

The next part of the process is to praise your kids for a job well done.

When they take on a tough challenge and could have gone for the easy option, let them know you value their choice. When they think about and learn from a setback, tell them well done. When they receive some tough feedback but you see them using it to improve, make sure you tell them you're proud of them. When they practise in their own time, let them know that was a great choice.

The more you praise behaviours, the more likely they are to be repeated.

Follow-up

Finally, don't forget what you talked about (write it down if it helps). Consistently learning from red dot moments will take time and it's easy to slip into old habits. Keep asking how things are going and if there's anything you can do to help.

Red dot moments will happen. Use simple questions to find out what your kids think about what happened and then help them commit to do something to be better next time.

THEY'RE WATCHING YOU

THIS IS THE shortest chapter in the book but probably the most important in terms of recognising how much parents can influence the behaviours of their kids. Have a look at the quote below from Angela Duckworth's book, *Grit: The Power of Passion and Perseverance*:

> *"First ask how much passion and perseverance you have for your own life goals. Then ask yourself how likely it is that your approach to parenting encourages your child to emulate you."*

Whether it's how much time and effort you put into developing yourself as a parent or how committed you are in the pursuit of other life goals, your kids will be watching you.

Enough said.

SELECTION

I'm just back from an under-17 football match my son was playing in and it convinced me that I need to have a separate chapter on the most common red dot moment kids and their parents will face.

I'm talking of course about selection and the understanding that with selection comes the potential for non-selection and deselection.

What put this in my mind was hearing (overhearing to be more precise!) a parent from the opposing team telling one of 'our' parents that their son was waiting to find out if he would be offered an academy contract for next season. These parents didn't seem to know each other but within about 15 seconds of their conversation starting their discussion had turned to selection.

Parents often ask me about how to handle the ups and downs of selection and it's probably the area where parents have the biggest potential to do more harm than good. The reason I say that is because, as kids grow and try to find their own identity, being selected or deselected for something can have a major impact on their self-esteem.

As a parent, you really feel for them and want to do

all you can to help. But what makes it much harder for kids to see the positives is if you (and also other family members and friends) are too focused on a selection outcome your kids can't control – "*are you in the team?*", "*when do you think you will get into the academy?*", "*when will you find out if you've been selected for the national championships?*".

Your kids will want to make you happy and if they think this hinges on a selection outcome, it can lead to them blaming others for what happened rather than taking responsibility or dropping out altogether as they found the disappointment (theirs and yours) too hard to deal with.

So as a parent one of the most important things you can do to help your kids is **NOT** to overly focus on the outcome of the selection.

Instead, treat selection and deselection like any other red dot moment by asking great questions . . .

"*Fantastic, you've worked really hard and I'm proud of you for being selected. What opportunities to keep developing your skills will this give you?*"

"*That is a blow as it would have been a great opportunity to get some feedback from coaches in the national squad. What else could you do to get that sort of feedback?*"

But you will need to work a little bit harder in these conversations because sometimes the things kids miss out on by not being selected really have an impact on their development and are hard to compensate for (I'm thinking for example about the chance to travel overseas to compete against unfamiliar opposition rather than missing out on a tracksuit or some free kit!). But you do need to help them try to find a way and stop them becoming too focused on how fair or unfair the decision was.

Good news and bad news around selection will happen. Your kids won't always think it's fair and sometimes they will be right and sometimes they will be wrong.

As a parent, you have a chance to help your kids recognise and take opportunities to improve if they are selected or try and create their own opportunities if they aren't. Take this chance and avoid focusing on how fair or unfair you thought the decision was. Instead keep asking, *"OK, this has happened, what are they going to do now?"*

THE POWER OF YET

THOSE OF YOU who know Carol Dweck's work on Mindset will be very familiar with the word YET. It's a great parenting word that can be added quite easily at the end of many of your kids' sentences.

"But I can't do it Mum."

"Not true son, you just can't do it YET."

Now I do love the word YET and have used it often myself. But there is a bit more to it than just adding it onto the end of your kids' sentences.

There are two reasons why someone can't do something YET. Either they haven't spent enough time practising, or what they're doing to improve won't actually lead to success (they need a better learning process). Adding the word YET works well if what they need to do is spend more time practising – *"You can't do it YET. Getting good will take time – when's the next chance you have to work on this?"*

However, if there's a chance that what they're doing won't lead to success then YET won't be enough (imagine how demotivating it could be if someone spends hours working hard on a process that doesn't lead to success). They need feedback.

In the same way that we can't just say to kids, "*believe in yourself, you can do it*", we also can't say "*don't worry, you just can't do it YET*", without helping them understand WHY they can't do it YET.

And while this is most often the role of the coach, we will see in the next chapter that sometimes parents are in the best position to develop this understanding.

HOW TO GIVE FEEDBACK

THERE WILL BE times when your kids won't be able to think everything through without some ideas and guidance. If they're not sure what to do, speaking to their coach is always a good option. But there will be times when this isn't possible so it's important for parents to learn how to provide feedback.

We've already looked at how to praise your kids when things go well, but what's the best way for parents to provide feedback when kids are missing a learning opportunity? Have a look at the process below:

1. Start with a guided question

2. Find out more about what they think

3. Add in your feedback or idea as an 'option'

4. Make sure they commit to do something

5. Follow up on progress

This approach is easy to use because you still focus on

asking great questions. The only difference is to add in your feedback or any ideas as an 'option'. What I mean by this is, try and avoid, "*I think you should . . .*" and instead make sure it comes across as "*what do you think about trying . . . ?*"

The best way to show you how to do this is to give you some real-life examples. Here's something that happened to me yesterday to get you started.

My 16-year-old son is very committed to football and although training and matches have taken a break over Christmas, he still trains on his own most days. Because we've talked about it before, I know he feels developing his speed endurance (the ability to do repeated sprints with short recovery) will be crucial in future and he knows he needs to work on it now – the future depends on what you do in the present.

To do this he does 'box-to-box' running sessions – running 90 metres at about 90% of top speed, stopping and turning and then running back to the start at the same speed. He then rests for 1 minute then repeats. This replicates the type of running he does in a game, getting up and down the pitch. It's also very hard work.

As always, I ask him what he will be doing each day in his own training and over a few days there were lots of gym and skills sessions but 'box-to-box' never seemed to be on his agenda. I had some feedback I was keen to share with him.

Here's what happened next.

"*Son, can I have a chat about the training you've been doing over Christmas?*"

"No problem, Dad."

"You've talked to me a lot about the importance of box-to-box sessions? (At this point a big smile appears on his face as he knows he's been rumbled.) I was just wondering if they're part of the plan over the next few days?"

"Definitely."

"How come you haven't already, you did tell me you felt this was important?"

"It is, I'm not really sure why."

Decision time. Do I tell him I think he's being lazy? This is where knowing your son or daughter is crucial to what you say next. My son isn't lazy and I felt this was more about his planning and I wondered if he hadn't yet found the best time to get the most out of this type of session.

"I know you're planning to train tomorrow. Is there an opportunity to do this type of running when you do your skills work?"

"Good idea, I'm up at the pitch anyway and I could do some ball work when I'm recovering to see how my skills hold up when I'm tired."

"I need to be up that way tomorrow at 9 a.m. (I didn't, but a little bit of help with time management is often useful for teenagers!), do you want a lift?"

"Yes please."

"No problem, I'm looking forward to hearing how it goes when I get home."

If you provide feedback in this way you're still able

to get your point across (I think you're missing an opportunity to do important fitness work) but in a way that encourages your kids to take time to think about the options and try and come up with their own solution.

Making sure they commit to do something (adding a box-to-box session into a skills session tomorrow) is important so you can follow up to see how it's gone. Once it becomes a habit you will need to ask them about it less, but that can take a bit of time.

Here's another example.

My 11-year-old son does lots of different sports including going to an after-school athletics club once a week. He's had great success in cross country running races but other kids are now beating him and now he doesn't want to compete in races (something he really used to enjoy).

"Can I ask you about running son and why you don't want to go to races anymore?"

"Sure, Dad."

"You used to love it and now don't want to go back – why is that?"

"I just don't like it anymore."

"What has changed to make you not like it?"

"Nothing, I just don't enjoy it."

I didn't say this was going to be easy – don't give up!

"One thing which has changed is that you're not winning every race this year – how does that make you feel?"

"I don't really mind about the result but I get

embarrassed because my friends expect me to win and keep asking me why I didn't?"

"Does that stop you wanting to go to races?"

"I think so."

"You know me and your Mum are not interested in how you compare to others. Do you think you're letting what your friends might say stop you from doing something you enjoy?"

"I think it does."

"What do you want to do about the next race – are you happy to go and have some fun and see if you can just ignore what your friends might say?"

"That sounds good, and can we stop for ice cream on the way home?"

"Good idea – it will give us a chance to talk about how it went."

This is a tricky scenario which is easier to address because you know your own kids. I thought he might be embarrassed (we talk to him a lot about not focusing on the result and having a race plan to work on to measure his progress) and I wanted him to recognise that the influence of his 'friends' was probably behind him missing out on something he enjoyed.

Having been through it before he will be more prepared for their comments next time and I'm looking forward to asking him what he's learned.

As I mentioned in the opening paragraph, coaches are the main source of feedback for young athletes. But you can see in both the examples above that the coach is not always around or aware of what young athletes might be thinking so parents can also play an important role in providing feedback.

The key to doing this well is to let them see your feedback as an **option they can think about** rather than **a statement they might choose to ignore**.

MONOSYLLABISM

WHAT CAN YOU do if your kids don't want to talk about it? Or they grunt one-word answers that are getting you nowhere? Surely that would never happen, right?

This can be tough, especially during puberty when hormones can make kids less willing to *share*, and it's another reason why it's so important to have a clear understanding between parents and kids about roles and responsibilities. Our kids know that their involvement in sport is a choice. They have no choice about eating well and exercising (getting their five-a-day and walking to school is a non-negotiable in our house!) but the sports they do are their choice.

My wife and I are very committed to support them in their choices and invest our own time, energy and money in the process. Our kids get this and appreciate it. They also get that we have a role to play in helping them learn and our questions are designed to do that. They know this because we've talked about it.

Are there times when our kids don't want to talk? Absolutely. You know your own kids and you'll know when to ask questions and when to leave it until later.

But they need to know your questions are part of the deal and monosyllabism is not an option!

WHAT WOULD YOU DO IF . . .

THE FINAL THING to do in the practical section of this book is to encourage you to practise. First, a quick reminder of what you're trying to do . . .

1. Help your kids understand more about ability and WHY they can be successful.

2. Help your kids take responsibility for their own learning.

3. Help your kids recognise and choose the behaviours that lead to success.

You can use great questions, feedback and praise to help you and from experience, these are skills you 'learn by doing'. Try, reflect, adapt and then try again. I still don't feel I get it right every time but I'm 100% committed to keep improving. The only way to do this is practice.

Here are a couple of examples of situations that can happen in sport and how a parent might handle them. This will get you thinking about using what you've learned with your own kids.

A young runner has been going to an athletics club and has made some good friends. The club has recently moved some kids to a more challenging training group but the young runner hasn't been moved and their friends have. They tell their parent about it on the way home.

Parent: How did that make you feel?

Runner: I felt embarrassed because everyone else got moved up except me.

Parent: Why do you think you weren't moved up this time?

Runner: I don't know.

Parent: Why do you think the others were moved up?

Runner: I'm not sure, they did join the club before me and I think they've all been running longer than me.

Parent: That make sense because remember people develop at different rates and it takes time to get good. You only come to the club once a week, is there anything you can do in your own time that would help you improve?

Runner: My coach did show us a session we could do on our own that would help.

Parent: When could you try that?

Runner: Maybe tomorrow after school?

Parent: Great idea – that sounds like a good plan and I can help you if you like. Well done.

A young football player goes to a tournament and plays really well, scores loads of goals and is the main reason why their team wins the tournament. They're buzzing on the way home.

Player: I'm so happy we won – look at my trophy! My coach said if they had a player of the tournament I would have won it.

Parent: That is a nice trophy – why do you think you were able to play so well today?

Player: I'm not sure – I've just always been good at football.

Parent: How old do you think you were when you started playing?

Player: I think when I was about six and then I joined the club when I was eight.

Parent: That's a long time – what have you worked on the most?

Player: My technique and endurance mostly – we spend ages working on that.

Parent: And I know you spend a lot of time working on your skills at home which I think is awesome. Do you think that helped you today?

Player: Definitely.

Parent: It looks like all the hard work and extra training you are doing is paying off. Well done, you should be proud.

Player: Thanks, Mum.

These are just a couple of examples of how you might handle these types of situations. Because you know your kids you will have a good idea of the type of approach that will work best for you. It's impossible to know what your kids will come out with when you ask them questions and it may well take more than one conversation to get to the bottom of what's going on. But keep persevering. Try, reflect, adapt and then try again. It works I promise.

Now have a look at the scenarios below and play through in your mind how you could use great questions, feedback and praise to help make sure your son or daughter learns as much as possible from each situation.

Scenario 1:
Someone at your club has been selected for a national squad training camp. Your son/daughter has predominantly beaten them in competitions but hasn't been selected and feels it's really unfair.

Scenario 2:
Your son/daughter has been invited to a trial match for their regional team. They really want to be selected and are super nervous on the way there and tell you they're worried their nerves will make them play poorly.

Scenario 3:
Your son/daughter has an opportunity to attend an overseas training camp. This would be the first time they have been away from home without you and although they've previously told you this would be a great opportunity, they don't want to go on the camp.

Scenario 4:
Your son/daughter has a lot going on at the moment including a ton of homework, a couple of parties and a big competition. They are feeling the pressure and want to skip a few training sessions over the next couple of weeks.

Hopefully that was useful. Now go and practise for real!

THE ELEPHANT IN THE ROOM

Our deepest fear is not that we are inadequate.
Our deepest fear is that we are powerful beyond measure . . .

Marianne Williamson

These are the first two lines from Marianne Williamson's poem 'Our Deepest Fear' and hopefully having read this book you will see that we all have the potential to be . . . powerful beyond measure. We really are capable of amazing things.

But with this understanding comes responsibility. In the same way our kids can excel at their chosen sport, **you can excel at supporting their learning.**

The good news is **you will already be doing many of the things mentioned in this book** and hopefully I've been able to help you understand WHY they're important so you keep doing them.

I'm also hoping that you embrace the things you're not so good at, or would like to change and work on those. We are creatures of habit and to improve, we need to recognise what we need to change, create a new process that is more effective than the old one and then consistently try, review, adapt and try again.

This can be tough but hopefully by understanding that . . .

1. We all develop at different rates

2. ALL skills can be developed

3. It takes time (and motivation)

4. We need to take responsibility

5. Behaviours are crucial

6. We can't do it on our own

. . . you know this is possible and commit to create the habits that work for you. Our kids need our help and you will need help too. To be successful at supporting the learning of your kids you also need people to support you to . . .

1. Understand more about ability and WHY you can be successful

2. Take responsibility for your own learning

3. Recognise and choose the behaviours that lead to success

. . . by asking you great questions, giving you feedback and praising you for a job well done.

My wife and I work as a team and I would encourage you to find someone who can give you the support and feedback you need to become an even more exceptional parent.

It won't be easy and you need to learn by doing and find the motivation to keep practising. But you can do it. I wish you good luck.

A FINAL THOUGHT . . .

I'M GUESSING YOU chose this book because your kids love sport and you want to do all you can to help them reach their potential. Although the examples in the book are all sporting examples, the same process applies to how you support the learning of your kids in whatever they do, be that sport, education, art, music, relationships, their occupation or anything else they feel passionate about.

These skills are transferable. The time you invest in this will pay dividends in a whole host of areas.

I now use what I've learned with my kids as much in education ("*I'm rubbish at maths*") and relationships ("*you'll never guess what happened at school today . . .*") as I do in sport. I also use these skills every day in my job. It helps me understand my clients and how I can help them. It also helps me to embrace the skills I need to future-proof and keep ahead of the competition.

But most of all I feel it helps me to help others understand **how to bring the best out of themselves**.

If you're looking for motivation to get started, I'm not sure I could offer you anything more powerful than that.

SHARED LEARNING

GOOD, BAD OR indifferent, please let me know what you found has worked well for you and any thoughts and comments on how we can keep improving the practical part of this book. I would love to hear from you so please drop me an email to feedback@stangerpro.com

Interested in regular tips and ideas about how to help your kids reach their potential in sport? Sign up to our free monthly Parents Top Tips email by visiting our website – www.stangerpro.com – in our resources section under Parents Top Tips. We also regularly publish articles to encourage you to think more deeply about how to create effective talent systems in any organisation so if this is of interest please sign up for our free monthly **Insights** email by visiting – www.stangerpro.com and clicking **Insights**. You can also follow us on Twitter @stangerpro

ACKNOWLEDGEMENTS

THERE ARE SO many people who have helped shape the insights in this book, there really are too many to mention – among them coaches past and present, fellow players, colleagues, clients, family and friends. However, special thanks to Ralph Campbell, Anne Kelly, Shirley Lumsden and my mum Elizabeth for reading countless drafts of the book and offering crucial feedback and support. I would also like to thank Pete Burns and the team at Polaris Publishing for their guidance and support in taking *Red Dot Parenting* to a wider audience.

I have faced a few red dot moments of my own in writing this book and a special thank you to my lovely wife Bid who has supported, questioned and challenged me throughout this process. A huge part of what you read is thanks to her.

Finally, my love and thanks to our awesome kids, Rosie, George and Jack. They support my learning as I (on a good day!) support theirs. Never a dull moment!

NOTES

NOTES

NOTES

NOTES

NOTES

NOTES

NOTES